IN THE MIDDLE COLONIES

HOW WE LIVED...

IN THE MIDDLE MIDDLE COLONIES

by Deborah Kent

BENCHMARK BOOKS

MARSHALL CAVENDISH
NEW YORK

ACKNOWLEDGMENT

For his generous assistance and expert advice, the author wishes to thank Clarence G. Seckel, Jr., Curriculum Coordinator in the Social Studies, East Saint Louis School District 189, East Saint Louis, Illinois.

Benchmark Books
Marshall Cavendish Corporation
99 White Plains Road
Tarrytown, New York 10591-9001

• • •

Library of Congress Cataloging-in-Publication Data
Kent, Deborah
In the middle colonies / Deborah Kent
p. cm—(How we lived)
Includes bibliographical references and index.
Summary: Discusses the history, social life, and customs of the various immigrant groups who settled in the middle colonies during the seventeenth and eighteenth centuries.
ISBN 0-7614-0907-6 (lib.bdg.)
1. Middle Atlantic States—History—Colonial period, ca. 1600-1775—Juvenile literature.
2. Middle Atlantic States—Social life and customs—17th century—Juvenile literature.
3. Middle Atlantic States—Social life and customs—18th century—Juvenile literature.   4. Frontier and pioneer life—Middle Atlantic States—Juvenile literature.   5. Pioneers—Middle Atlantic States—History—Juvenile literature
[1. Middle Atlantic State—History—Colonial period, ca. 1600-1775.   2. Middle Atlantic States—Social life and customs.
3. Frontier and pioneer life—Middle Atlantic States.   4. Pioneers.]   I. Title.   II. Series.
E162.K33   2000   98-23097   974'.02—dc21   CIP   AC

• • •

Printed in Hong Kong
3 5 6 4

• • •

Book Designer: Judith Turziano
Photo Researcher: Debbie Needleman

• • •

PHOTO CREDITS

Front cover: Courtesy of the Colonial Williamsburg Foundation; pages 2–3: New York State Historical Association, Cooperstown, NY. Photo by Richard Walker; pages 6–7, 10–11, 14, 22, 28, 30–31, 33, 40–41, 47, 48, 50–51: North Wind Picture Archives; pages 12, 26, 44, 46: Stock Montage; page 13: D. Van Kirk / The Image Bank; page 16: Annie Griffiths Belt / Corbis; pages 20–21: Historical Picture Archive / Corbis; pages 25, 52: Colonial Williamsburg Foundation; page 32: Museum of Fine Arts, Boston, Bequest of Maxim Karolik, Acc# 64.456; pages 34, 36: Lee Snider / Corbis; page 39: Private Collection, Photograph courtesy of the Museum of American Folk Art, New York; page 43: Library of Congress / Corbis; page 54: Corbis / Bettmann; page 57: Collection of the Museum of American Folk Art, New York, Promised anonymous gift, P2. 1984.1; page 58: Historical Society of Pennsylvania, PA / Bridgeman Art Library, London / New York; page 59: Collection of the Museum of American Folk Art, New York, Museum of American Folk Art, Purchase, 1981. 12.4; page 60: Museum of Fine Arts, Boston, Gift of Mrs. Samuel Cabot, Acc# 40.79

Contents

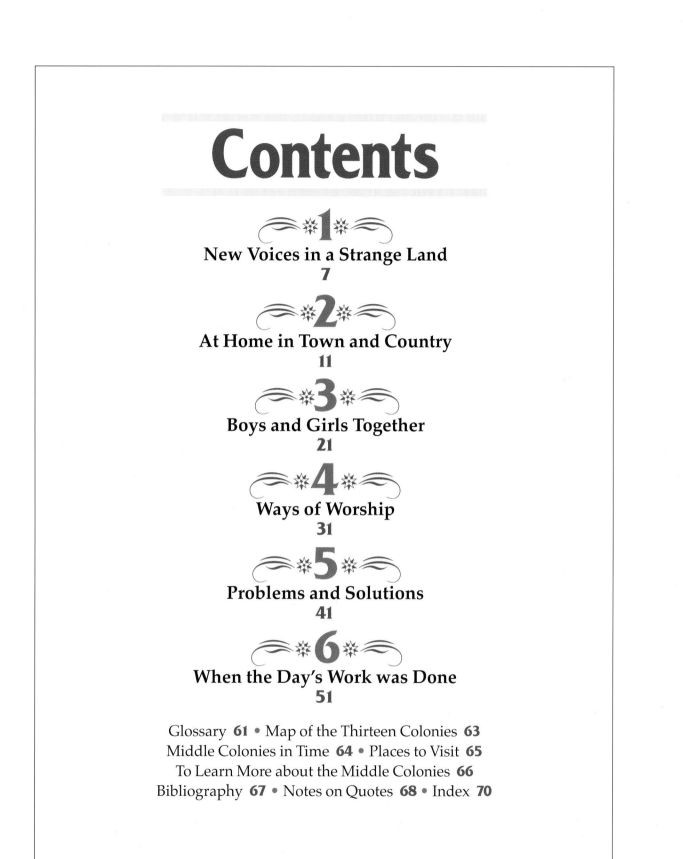

1
New Voices in a Strange Land

*"The air was sweet because the savages at this time
of the year burn the underbrush for hunting. The land
is full of sweet-scented herbs such as sassafras....
The fragrance drifts seaward, permitting the
land to be smelled before it is seen."*

—DAVID DE VRIES, A DUTCH MERCHANT,
ON A VISIT TO NEW AMSTERDAM IN THE 1630S

Writing in the 1630s, the Dutch merchant David de Vries remembered his first impressions of the land he knew as New Netherland. At the heart of New Netherland, the Dutch settlement of New Amsterdam clung to the southern tip of Manhattan Island. With New Amsterdam as their base, the colonists fanned out to neighboring regions of New Jersey and Long Island.

The Dutch held New Netherland for barely forty years. In 1664 British warships aimed their cannons at New Amsterdam's fort. The Dutch gave up without a struggle. Under the British the territory received the name New York.

New York sprang up between two well-established British colonies. Massachusetts, to the north, was the hub of a group of colonies known as New England. To the south lay Virginia, whose first settlement was founded in 1607. The capture of New Netherland allowed the British to fill in the gap between these two strongholds. By the end of the 1600s they had established colonies in present-day New Jersey and across the Delaware River in Pennsylvania. To the south Delaware and Maryland completed the chain of English colonies along the Atlantic coast.

Because of their position between New England and Virginia, these settlements are often referred to as the Middle Colonies.

Although they were all governed by the British, each of the Middle Colonies had its own character. The first colonists in Pennsylvania were Quakers, members of a peace-loving religious sect that had been persecuted in England. Pennsylvania also attracted colonists from Germany. Swedish and Finnish settlers left their mark along Delaware Bay. Roman Catholics from England found religious freedom in Maryland. New York and northern New Jersey retained a strong Dutch flavor.

European immigrants were not the only people who influenced the development of the colonies. People from many parts of West Africa arrived against their will to live as slaves. The newcomers from Europe and Africa encountered Native Americans from many different tribes. These people were the "savages" mentioned by David de Vries.

In the early 1700s a visitor wrote that he heard eighteen different

GETTING THEIR MONEY'S WORTH

In 1624 Dutch fur traders established a thriving outpost at Fort Orange (present-day Albany) on the Hudson River. It was soon overshadowed by New Amsterdam, the Dutch settlement on Manhattan Island. In 1626 Peter Minuit, the governor of New Netherland, bought Manhattan from the Native Americans. In this legendary transaction the Indians received beads, blankets, and tools worth about twenty-four dollars today. After the British took control in 1664, the territory was renamed New York, in honor of the Duke of York, the brother of King Charles II. Graced by a fine, deep harbor, New York City became one of the most important seaports in the thirteen British colonies.

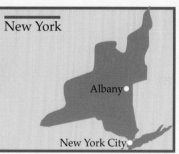

New York

Albany

New York City

languages spoken as he walked a Manhattan street. In the Middle Colonies people from many lands collided. At times the impact was shattering. But as the years passed, the colonists came to think of themselves not as Germans, Swedes, or Hollanders, but as Americans. In a land of challenge and possibilities they were building a new way of life.

2
At Home in Town and Country

"The Dutch here keep their houses very neat and clean, both without and within. Their chamber floors are generally laid with rough plank which, in time, by constant rubbing and scrubbing, becomes as smooth as if it had been planed. Their chambers and rooms are large and handsome. They have their beds generally in alcoves so that you may go through all the rooms of a great house and see never a bed."

—Dr. Alexander Hamilton, a Maryland physician, describing a visit to Albany, New York, in 1744

FROM GARRET TO CELLAR

By the 1740s the Middle Colonies were flourishing. The majority of the colonists lived on farms, which often clustered together to form villages. Thousands of other people lived in the port cities of New York and Philadelphia. In city or country, homes in the Middle Colonies were comfortable by the standards of the day.

In New Amsterdam, a young couple strolls past a Dutch colonial family relaxing on their stoop.

Life was far more harsh in the 1600s when the Middle Colonies were getting their start. The settlers faced the backbreaking task of carving farmland out of tangled forests. They lived in fear of attack from the Native Americans whose land they bought or stole. And they had to build shelters to protect themselves from the wind and snow.

The first Dutch colonists in New Amsterdam lived in rough "pit houses." They dug a pit about seven feet deep and lined it with timber and bark. Saplings and branches were woven together to form a roof. They plastered the roof with mud and thatched it with reeds. Cold, damp, and cheerless, these homes were a grim introduction to the new land.

Weather vanes were popular in colonial times.

By comparison, the homes of the Swedes and Finns on Delaware Bay were snug and warm. These colonists built sturdy cabins of logs, sealing the cracks with clay and moss. Eventually the log cabin became a symbol of the American frontier. Its origins lie in the forests of Scandinavia.

As soon as they could, the colonists built more substantial houses. Dutch homes were usually made of wood and had steep, tiled roofs. The roof was often crowned with a weather vane in the shape of a rooster, horse, or sailing ship. By observing which way the weather vane pointed, colonists could tell the direction of the wind.

In front of each house was a porch or stoop. On warm evenings families sat on their stoops, exchanging news with their neighbors. The stoop remained an important feature of houses in New York City well into the twentieth century.

The garret, the narrow space beneath the sloping roof, was often used for storing sausages and other smoked meats. The second floor of the house was reserved for bedrooms. The ground floor contained the *kamer* (parlor), a room reserved for special occasions such as weddings and funerals. The homemaker kept the *kamer* spotlessly clean. The floor was covered with a layer of fine white sand that was swept into precise patterns of diamonds or curves. Any mischievous child who dared to enter the parlor was sure to leave telltale footprints.

An essential part of every Dutch house was the cellar. Cool in summer and never too cold in winter, it was a perfect place for storing food. After the autumn harvest the cellar overflowed with potatoes, turnips, and

In colonial homes the family liked to gather near the warmth of the fire. Dutch colonists often decorated their large fireplaces with painted tiles.

A SPECIAL TREAT

Aspecial treat enjoyed by the German colonists in Pennsylvania was shoofly pie. The recipe is still popular in some parts of the state today. Give it a try.

SHOOFLY PIE

1/2 cup molasses

1 cup hot water

1 baked piecrust

1 1/2 cups flour

1 cup brown sugar

1/4 cup butter

Slowly add the molasses to the hot water and stir until smooth. Pour this mixture into the piecrust. Combine the flour, sugar, and butter in a large mixing bowl. Blend until the mixture is crumbly. Spread these crumbs on the molasses mixture and bake at 350 degrees Fahrenheit for about 20 minutes.

apples. Great barrels held pickles, salted fish, and spiced fruit; kegs held beer and ale. Clean water was in short supply, so everyone, even children, often drank beer with meals.

Of all the rooms in a colonial home, none was more important or better loved than the kitchen.

BESIDE THE ROARING FIRE

In 1685 Sally Brindley, a Quaker girl in Bucks County, Pennsylvania, wrote to her grandmother in England. "I wish thee could see our big kitchen, Sally wrote. "It has a fireplace entirely across one end of the room. Papa brings the backlog in with the horse, and when the boys pile up wood against it, such a fire as it does make!"

Colonial cooks hung heavy iron pots from the lugpole and cooked their food over the open flame. This photograph shows what a kitchen was like in colonial Pennsylvania.

As Sally Brindley describes, the fireplace in a colonial kitchen was enormous. It was big enough to hold an immense "backlog" that might be a foot or more thick. The backlog could burn for several days. Chairs and benches clustered on the tiled hearth in front of the blaze. There the family sat, warm and cozy, on winter evenings. When cold winds howled, the kitchen was the only comfortable room in the house.

Between two ledges at the rear of the fireplace stretched the "lugpole." Pots and kettles could be hung above the flames from this long, sturdy beam. Breads and pies were baked in a "Dutch oven," a heavy iron pot on thick legs. The pot stood in the fireplace on the glowing coals. When the lid was closed, more coals were piled on top. The cook removed the pies or steaming loaves with a long-handled shovel-like utensil called a peel.

In the early days of the colonies, metal and china tableware were almost unknown. People ate from carved wooden dishes called trenchers. By the 1700s most families in the Middle Colonies had begun to use pewter dishes and mugs. Pewter is a metal formed by blending a small amount of copper and antimony with tin. Pewter dishes were not strong and would start to melt if placed too close to the fire. But they had a cheerful shine that helped to brighten the kitchen.

Homemakers in the Middle Colonies proudly showed off their best kitchenware. Pewter mugs and bowls, blue and white china dishes from the Netherlands, and perhaps a cherished silver pitcher were arranged on the shelves of a kitchen cupboard. Dutch families sometimes had a hanging wooden rack for spoons.

In general the colonists liked to eat foods they had enjoyed at home in Europe. Dutch and German settlers loved salt pork, pickles, and sausage. Colonists from England preferred mutton, chicken, and beef. But all of the colonists acquired a taste for the foods they discovered in their new home. One new delicacy was pigeon pie. Every year vast flocks of passenger pigeons passed through the colonies on their spring and fall migrations. These flocks were so dense that a child with a stick could knock birds out of the trees.

Seafood also delighted the colonists. Early accounts describe shellfish of unimaginable size. Oysters from Chesapeake Bay measured a foot long. A single blue crab could feed four hungry men. Some reports claim that New York Bay was home to enormous lobsters. According to these records the lobsters were six feet in length from the tail to the mighty snapping pincers. These monsters had died out by 1775—if they ever existed at all.

PEACOCKS AND SPARROWS

In 1772 a Philadelphia newspaper printed a mocking description of a typical man of fashion. "The hair is loaded with powder and pomade…. The rest [of his attire] chiefly consists of French silk, gold lace, fringe, silk stockings, a hat and feather and sometimes a cockade…. [He has] white hands, a diamond ring, a snuff-box, a scented handkerchief, and a cane."

A BARREL TAPPED AT BOTH ENDS

Benjamin Franklin once said that New Jersey was "a barrel tapped at both ends." Its farms fed two big, hungry cities: New York and Philadelphia. In about 1630 Dutch settlers founded an outpost called Pavonia at what is now Jersey City. Swedish fur traders settled in southern New Jersey in 1638. In 1655 the Dutch drove the Swedes out of New Jersey. The Dutch lost control to the English in 1664.

Part of MA

NH
NY MA
CT RI
PA
NJ
MD DE
VA
NC
SC
GA

The Thirteen Colonies

Atlantic Ocean

Gulf of Mexico

New Jersey
Jersey City
Perth Amboy
Stanhope
Trenton
Burlington

Such style-conscious men were known as dandies. In newly built colonial cities such as Philadelphia and New York, they tried to follow the high fashions of faraway Europe.

Stylish women dressed in colorful gowns trimmed with lace, ribbons, and embroidery. Beneath their gowns they wore several layers of petticoats that rustled as they walked. In their dainty shoes of silk or satin they didn't walk very far. Ladies' footwear was not designed for the rutted, muddy streets of a colonial town. When they went out, women strapped thick wooden soles to the bottoms of their shoes. These extra soles gave some protection from the mud.

Colonial ladies wore their hair in elaborate styles. It could be curled, braided, or piled on top of the head. Often it was dusted with white powder. Men wore powdered wigs that came in endless shapes and sizes. Wigs were hot and uncomfortable, and the powder left a messy film on clothing and furniture. Such was the price of staying in style.

Not all of the colonists dressed like these fashionable peacocks. The wives and daughters of Dutch farmers wore long, full skirts and white kerchiefs over their shoulders. A Dutch woman of New York or New Jersey often wore a heavy brass chain around her waist. From this chain, or *chatelaine,* hung a jangling assortment of scissors, keys, and pincushions. In this case, the fashion was also practical.

One group of colonists refused to wear fancy clothes of any kind. The Quakers who settled in Pennsylvania believed that dress should be as simple as possible. The most devout Quakers avoided bright colors and dressed chiefly in grays and browns. Compared to the dandies of fashion, they were humble sparrows.

Whether they were rich or poor, Quaker or Dutch, colonial children dressed much like their parents. Childhood was usually brief in the colonies. At an early age many children were expected to carry the responsibilities of adults.

3

Boys and Girls Together

"I have not read of any virtue birch hath in physic, howbeit it serveth many good uses, and none better than for the beating of stubborn boys, that either lie or will not learn."

—FROM A BOOK ON HERBAL MEDICINE POPULAR
IN THE COLONIES IN THE SEVENTEENTH CENTURY

SCHOOL DAYS

By today's standards boys and girls in the Middle Colonies didn't have much fun. They spent much of their time doing household chores or helping with farmwork. In addition, many were sent to work away from home. Nevertheless, colonial children managed to play and laugh as children do everywhere.

Many children in the Middle Colonies never had a chance to attend school. Schoolhouses stood only in the larger villages and towns. Most boys who did attend school completed their studies by the age of twelve.

Schoolmasters often punished children by embarrassing them.
In addition to the dunce cap, lazy students might be made to wear signs
around their necks, such as "Baby Good-for-Nothing" or "Idle Boy."

During the 1600s girls were seldom sent to school at all.

A few women taught school in the colonies, but most schoolmasters were men. In many communities the schoolmaster was not highly respected. He was considered to be little better than a hired farmhand. Some schoolmasters were drifters, who wandered from town to town, working for a few months, getting into trouble, and moving on. A notice in the Maryland Gazette reads: "Ran away: A servant man who followed the occupation of a schoolmaster, much given to drinking and gambling."

The schoolmaster had many duties besides teaching. In New York and New Jersey he rang the church bells on Sundays. He led the congregation in singing hymns. He was also the official "consoler of the sick," and he even dug graves. His salary was not paid in money. The family of each pupil paid an agreed-upon number of cheeses, beaver pelts, or bushels of corn.

Most schoolmasters in the Middle Colonies were strict disciplinarians. Pupils were whipped for misbehaving or for failing to learn their lessons. One notorious Pennsylvania schoolmaster earned the nickname "Tiptoe Bobby." He prowled the room with a raccoon's furry tail in his hand. The tail was weighted with stones at one end. If he spied a pupil yawning or fidgeting, he would fling the tail at the offending pupil's head.

Many schoolmasters used shame as a form of punishment. In New Netherland a child who didn't study was ridiculed as a "dunce," or fool. The schoolmaster forced the pupil to stand on a stool wearing a pointed hat called a dunce cap. The other children in the room were encouraged to laugh at the dunce's disgrace.

Some parents tried to make sure that schoolmasters would treat their children gently. The contract for a teacher on Long Island in 1682 required him to "demean himself friendly and patient toward the children." In New Amsterdam a schoolmaster lost control of his pupils when the parents forbade him to lay his hands on them. He complained that the children "beat each other and tore the clothes from each other's backs."

The schoolhouse in the Middle Colonies was made of logs and was often hexagonal, or six-sided. The desks were planks that jutted from the log walls like shelves. When they worked at these desks, the pupils faced the walls, their backs to the teacher.

The school day began and ended with a prayer. In between, the children spent their time reciting from memory or working long problems in arithmetic. Only on rare occasions did some special event break the monotony. In 1739 Mary Grafton Dulany, a thirteen-year-old girl from Delaware, wrote to her father from boarding school in Philadelphia. Her letter describes an occasion much like an awards assembly of today. "I went to Madame B.'s exhibition. There were five Crowns [awards of high honor].… They were crowned in great style in the assembly rooms in the presence of 500 spectators."

THE WORKADAY WORLD

"This indenture witnesses that William Mathews, son of Marrat of the city of New York, a widow,…does voluntarily and of his own free will and accord and by the consent of his said mother put himself as an apprentice cordwainer to Thomas Windover of the city aforesaid." When he signed this contract in October 1718, William Mathews bound himself to Thomas Windover for seven years. During that time he would have to "serve his master, faithfully keep his secrets, [and] gladly obey his lawful commands." In return Thomas Windover, the master, promised to teach William the cordwainer's, or shoemaker's, trade. He would even send William to school for three months every winter.

All over the colonies children as young as nine or ten were bound out as apprentices. The apprentice lived as a servant in the master's house. The master provided all of the apprentice's food and clothing. If the master was kind, the apprentice was treated as a member of the family. But some apprentices fell into the hands of cruel masters who treated them harshly.

Though it sometimes led to abuses, the apprentice system had a great deal to offer. It enabled young people to learn a practical trade that could support them. Boys apprenticed to carpenters, joiners (furniture makers), coopers (barrel makers), bakers, or barbers. Girls were bound out to

Everyone in colonial America needed barrels for storing or shipping goods. So becoming an apprentice to a cooper was a smart career choice. Here is what a colonial barrel maker's workshop might have been like.

seamstresses or milliners (makers of hats). When the apprentice's term of service was over, the master was supposed to give him or her a bit of a start in life. According to his indenture contract, William Mathews was to receive "a sufficient new suit of apparel, four shirts, and two necklets [detachable collars]."

Throughout colonial America, families were large. This was certainly true in the Middle Colonies. It was common for a child to have a dozen or more brothers and sisters. Children were seen as family assets. They were expected to help their parents inside and outside the home. Scarcely any task was reserved for adults only.

In general girls and boys had different chores. Girls cooked, mended, and cared for their younger siblings. Farm boys worked with their fathers in the fields. A boy who lived in town ran errands or served customers in his parents' shop.

Children also earned money for the family by working at home in "cottage industries." Girls as young as six learned to operate a spinning wheel. Found in nearly every colonial home, the spinning wheel turned woolen or flax fibers into thread. Flax is a graceful plant whose dried stems resemble straw. Thread made from flax often was sold to a weaver, who turned it into linen cloth. But some families did their own weaving as well as spinning. Children learned to help with the complex process of working on a large wooden loom.

Boys brought in extra cash by trapping and skinning beavers,

Candle making was a cottage industry in which children often worked. Pieces of fat, or tallow, had to be melted in an iron kettle. Then the wicks were dipped into the hot fat and hung from a rack to dry. This step was repeated many times until the candles were the right size.

LEAVE IT TO BEAVER

Trapping beavers for their fur was big business in the colonies. But some colonists kept beavers as pets. Peter Kalm, a Swedish naturalist who visited the colonies, reported, "Some persons in Philadelphia have tamed beavers so that they go fishing with them, and they always come back to their masters."

muskrats, foxes, and other fur-bearing animals. A pelt in good condition fetched a handsome price. Most boys enjoyed being outdoors. Tramping through the woods to check their traps was more like play than work.

COASTING BOARDS AND FLANDERS DOLLS

The Netherlands is a remarkably flat country. Some of the Dutch colonists who came to the New World had probably never seen a hill before. It did not take long, however, for Dutch children to discover the joys of a hillside covered with snow. Coasting downhill on homemade sleds became a favorite winter pastime. Many grown-ups frowned on coasting as rowdy behavior. In 1728 the city of Albany even passed a law stating that all sleds should be seized by the constable and broken to bits.

Ice-skating had been a popular pastime in the Netherlands. The frozen lakes and ponds of New York and New Jersey became skating rinks for colonial children. Teenagers looked forward to skating parties, when they could glide over the ice in pairs. Ice skates consisted of iron blades strapped to a pair of sturdy shoes.

Children in the Middle Colonies played with many of the same toys that children enjoy today. They flew kites and spun wooden tops. The wealthiest girls and boys had a variety of windup mechanical toys imported from Europe. Many girls also had "Flanders dolls" in elegant dresses.

The Dutch brought ninepins to the New World. The game became so popular that some colonies had it banned. But that didn't stop people from playing. They simply added another piece to the game and changed the name to tenpins. Today, it's called bowling.

These dolls were originally sent to dressmakers in the colonies to show the latest European fashions. When they outlived this role they became the treasured playthings of little girls.

Looping a piece of string over their fingers, colonial children played cat's cradle, a game that is still well known. In colonial times the game was called cratch-cradle, from a Dutch word meaning crèche. The intricate loops of string were meant to represent the manger where the Christ Child lay.

Some games were played by adults as well as children. Ninepins, a form of bowling, was popular with young and old. "Tick-tack," a board game that used dice and moveable tiles, also appealed to all ages.

Children were especially fond of vigorous outdoor sports. "Football" was a rough-and-tumble game resembling soccer. The game of "stone-poison," popular in and around Philadelphia, was a form of tag. The players had to jump from one stone to another. A player became "it" if his or her foot touched the ground.

Work, play, and study were not the only occupations of children in the Middle Colonies. Children and adults spent many hours each week in church. Religion was a central and guiding force in colonial life.

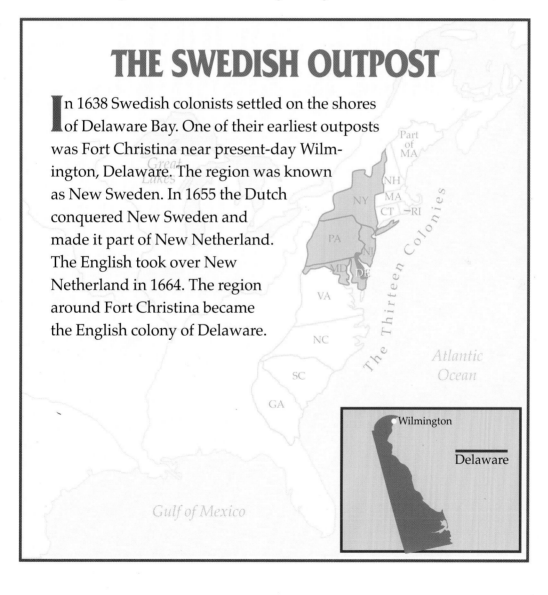

THE SWEDISH OUTPOST

In 1638 Swedish colonists settled on the shores of Delaware Bay. One of their earliest outposts was Fort Christina near present-day Wilmington, Delaware. The region was known as New Sweden. In 1655 the Dutch conquered New Sweden and made it part of New Netherland. The English took over New Netherland in 1664. The region around Fort Christina became the English colony of Delaware.

4
Ways of Worship

"God, through Christ, has placed a principle in every man to inform him of his duty, and to enable him to do it; and those that live up to that principle are the people of God; and those that live in disobedience to it are not God's people."

—WILLIAM PENN, LEADER OF THE QUAKERS IN PENNSYLVANIA, 1696

TO TREMBLE BEFORE GOD

No paintings or stained-glass windows adorned the Quaker meetinghouses in Pennsylvania. No lofty church steeples pierced the sky. When Quakers gathered for worship on a Sunday morning they did not sing hymns or even listen to a sermon. Instead they sat together in silence, communing with God. From time to time someone in the congregation rose and spoke aloud. It might be a verse from the Bible, or an idea about how people should best live according to Scripture. The others listened with respect. Whatever was said in meeting was inspired by the Lord.

The Quakers were the first European settlers in Pennsylvania. They were members of the Society of Friends, a religious sect that was harshly persecuted in England. The Friends were known as Quakers because it was said that they quaked and trembled before the Almighty. The Quakers sought to live in humility and Christian love. They wore simple, plain clothes. They believed that all human beings were equal in the eyes of God. In the New World they tried to put their ideals into action.

Quakers believed the "Inward Light" made them tremble and moved them to rise and speak during Sunday meetings.

Under the leadership of William Penn, the Quakers treated the Native Americans more respectfully than did most other European colonists. As a result Pennsylvania enjoyed many decades of peace.

As time passed, many Quakers strayed from their principles. Some grew rich and built elegant houses in Philadelphia. The simple life was forgotten. One visitor to a Quaker family remarked with humor, "This plain Friend and his plain though pretty wife…provided us with the most costly entertainment, ducks, hams, chicken, beef, pig, tarts, cream, custards, jellies, trifles, beer, porter, punch, wine, and a long etcetera."

William Penn tried to deal fairly with the Indians, but he wasn't sure who they actually were. "I am ready to believe them of the Jewish Race," he wrote, "I mean, of the stock of the Ten Tribes."

A WELCOME TO ALL

Today in the United States we take for granted the right to worship as we choose. But governments in seventeenth-century Europe often told people what religion they must follow. The Middle Colonies offered something precious and unique: religious freedom. From England, France, Switzerland, and Germany, immigrants came to build their churches and live by their beliefs.

The Ephrata Cloister still stands today in southeastern Pennsylvania.

William Penn encouraged members of many religious groups to settle in Pennsylvania. The Moravians, a Protestant sect from Germany, established a thriving community around the town of Bethlehem. While the Quakers tended to go into business, most Moravians were farmers. Their stately stone houses and churches were built to last. The Moravians had a deep commitment to education. They founded some twenty schools, including the first boarding school for girls in the thirteen colonies.

The Seventh-Day Baptists were another Protestant group from Germany. Their community, or cloister, was centered at Ephrata in Lancaster County. Many members of this group remained celibate in order to devote their lives wholly to God. They believed that iron symbolized the forces of evil, so they used it as little as possible. Instead of using nails, they fastened furniture together with tightly fitting wooden pegs. The people of Ephrata did not even iron their clothing. Instead they pressed out wrinkles with hot blocks of wood.

Like Pennsylvania, Maryland granted freedom of worship to people of all faiths. Maryland was founded as a refuge for Roman Catholics, who were persecuted in Protestant England. Church bells in Annapolis called some to Protestant services and others to Mass.

Jews, too, were severely persecuted in Europe. In many places they were not allowed to own their own homes or businesses. Jewish immi-

COUNTING ONE'S BLESSINGS

To the people of Ephrata, almost everything held some religious meaning. Even the shapes of numbers were symbolic. A circle represented God, and a straight line stood for humankind. Thus the number 6 was to be avoided, because it placed humanity above God. The number 9 was preferred in measurements for buildings; in the 9 God was above humankind.

The bell tower of a typical Dutch Reformed church.

grants found new freedom in the Middle Colonies. In about 1750 the Swedish naturalist Peter Kalm wrote: "Many Jews have settled in New York.… They have a synagogue, own their dwelling houses…and are allowed to keep shops."

THE WORD OF THE *DOMINE*

On Sunday mornings in New Netherland the local schoolmaster went from house to house, banging on each door with a heavy stick. "Church time!" he called through the streets. "Church time!" When the congregation filed into the church, the schoolmaster led the opening prayer and hymns. Then at last the pastor, or *domine,* climbed the steps to the pulpit and began to preach. The *domine* was the most powerful member of the church community. And in New Netherland, the church and the state were closely bound together. Most of the colonists in New Netherland belonged to a Protestant sect called the Dutch Reformed Church. Throughout the colonial era the Dutch Reformed had a strong influence in New York and parts of New Jersey.

The first churches in New Netherland were square log structures with narrow slitlike windows. The men of the congregation carried their guns to the service. They were ready to fire from the windows in case of enemy attack. (At various times in the history of the colony the enemy consisted of Native Americans, the English, and, in northern New York, the French.)

Later Dutch Reformed churches were six- or eight-sided buildings made of wood or stone. At the peak of the steep roof perched a bell tower crowned with a weather vane. The bell rope hung down in the middle of the church, and was wrapped around a post when not in use.

Everyone who attended church sat in an assigned place. Indians and African Americans were restricted to the upper gallery. Families of high standing had special seats on the sides or near the front. The family paid the church for its seating privileges. The family pew passed from father to son like any other valuable property.

During the service a church official called a deacon walked down the aisle to take the collection. He carried a cloth contribution bag, or *sacje,* on the end of a slender pole. A little bell jingled as the deacon waved the *sacje* in front of each parishioner.

Sunday was treated with special respect under both the Dutch and the English. Neither work nor games were allowed on the Sabbath. Laws forbade "the ordinary and customary labors of callings, such as sowing, mowing, building, sawing wood, smithing, bleeching, hunting, [and] fishing." There were also laws against "dancing, card-playing, tick-

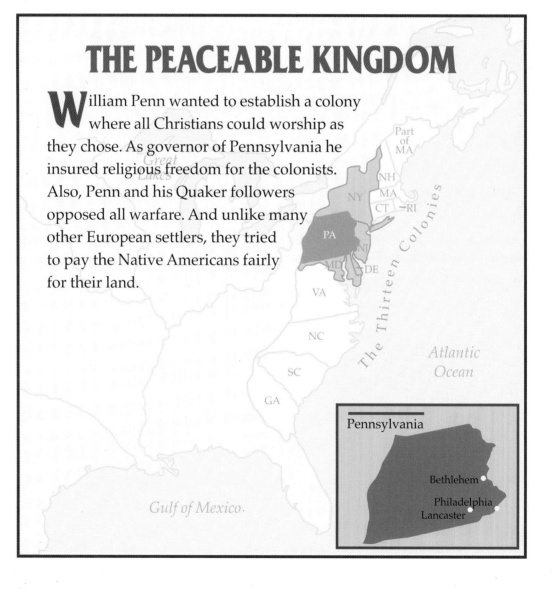

THE PEACEABLE KINGDOM

William Penn wanted to establish a colony where all Christians could worship as they chose. As governor of Pennsylvania he insured religious freedom for the colonists. Also, Penn and his Quaker followers opposed all warfare. And unlike many other European settlers, they tried to pay the Native Americans fairly for their land.

Pennsylvania

The Peaceable Kingdom *by Edward Hicks. Hicks believed*
William Penn's treaty with the Indians (pictured on the left) was
the first step toward a peaceable kingdom in the New World.

tacking, playing at ball, at bowls, at ninepins; taking jaunts in boats,
wagons, or carriages." Anyone who broke these laws was punished.
Fining was only one penalty the colonial authorities imposed. They also
found ingenious means to bring about public humiliation. Their methods
may seem cruel to us, but the colonists felt that harsh measures were
needed to keep society running smoothly.

5
Problems and Solutions

"No person shall strip the fences of posts or rails under penalty for the first offense of being whipped and branded, and for the second, of punishment with the cord until death ensues."

—A LAW PASSED IN NEW NETHERLAND IN 1659

THE WRONG SIDE OF THE LAW

Many offenses that seem trivial today, such as stealing fence posts, were taken very seriously in the Middle Colonies. Old court records bulge with cases of men and women prosecuted for calling a neighbor a "dough face", "pig," "talebearer," or even "black pudding." Slander was a punishable offense. So was any behavior that could be considered indecent. In New Amsterdam a woman named Grietje van Salee once accused Anneke Jans Bogardus, the *domine*'s wife, of lifting her petticoats to reveal her ankles as she crossed the street. Anneke brought witnesses who testified that she only raised her petticoats because the street was muddy. Anneke then accused Grietje of defaming her good character. The court found Grietje guilty. She was fined and forced to make a public apology. Her husband was also punished, for allowing her to make false statements. For a year and a day he was forbidden to carry his gun on the streets. In New Amsterdam, clinging to the edge of the wilderness, that was humiliation indeed.

Persons convicted of name-calling, drunkenness, or breaking the Sabbath were often sentenced to stand in the stocks. This device was a wooden frame with openings for the arms and legs. The convict stood imprisoned for days, in the rain and snow or under the baking sun. Passersby stopped to stare, jeer, or throw rotten vegetables.

A law in colonial Maryland stated that "a common scold may be indicted and if convicted shall be sentenced to be placed in a certain engine of correction called the trebucket, castigatory, or cuckingstool." This "engine of correction," best known as the "ducking stool," was a seat at the end of a sturdy pole. The "common scold," a woman accused of complaining or criticizing, was tied to the stool and lowered into the water. She would be held underwater for half a minute or more. The ducking stool was a punishment reserved exclusively for female offenders.

Males were not spared from harsh punishments. One penalty, popular among the Indians as well as the colonists, was running the gantlope or gauntlet. In 1681 a soldier named Melchoir Classen was court-martialed in New York for petty theft. The record states that "the said Melchoir Classen shall run the gantlope once, the length of the fort: where according to the custom of that punishment, the soldiers shall have switches delivered to them, with which they shall strike him as he passes between them stripped to the waist." At least Melchoir Classen got away with his life. Theft was often a capital crime. Thieves were sometimes hanged for stealing a few tools or coins.

For some convicts, colonial life itself was a sentence. Courts in Great Britain regularly banished prisoners to the New World. There they were forced to work out their sentences through several years of labor. At one

Punishments in colonial days, such as running the gauntlet, seem harsh to us today.

time nearly half of the colonists in Maryland were convicts. Few of these men and women were hardened criminals. They were simply poor people who had never had opportunities. Despite great hardships, many built successful lives in the colonies.

GOOD FENCES MAKE GOOD NEIGHBORS

In 1674 a neighbor's pigs and cows invaded a farmer's fields in New York. The animals trampled cornstalks and devoured the tender ears. The distraught farmer, Henry van Dyke, took his neighbor to court. The neighbor was forced to pay a heavy fine.

Fires broke out often in the colonies. To fight them, members of a community would quickly form a bucket brigade— a line of people who would pass buckets of water from hand to hand to put out the blaze. Here, colonial New Yorkers are using an early kind of pump.

Even in cities such as Philadelphia and New York, most colonists kept cows, pigs, chickens, and other livestock. Laws required them to control their animals and prevent them from doing damage. Strong fences were essential. No wonder the colonists passed stern laws against stealing posts and rails.

Actually there is no record that anyone was ever hanged for breaking down a fence. The colonists passed an endless series of laws about controlling livestock, but these rules were hard to enforce. In New York City wandering hogs posed a major problem. They frightened horses, knocked down pedestrians, and even attacked small children. But the pigs performed one valuable service: they ate much of the garbage people threw into the streets.

Roving pigs were not the ideal solution to the colonists' garbage problems. In 1657 a New Amsterdam law forbade "throwing of any rubbish, filth, oyster shells, dead animal or anything like it" into the streets. A garbage wagon passed once a week to haul the trash away. Each family had to pile its own refuse into the wagon. The system was less than perfect. Somehow the streets remained almost as dirty as before. Lazy colonists liked to heap their garbage in front of a neighbor's house, hoping it would become someone else's concern.

Fire prevention was another area that called for cooperation in the community. Fires often started in chimneys and spread swiftly from house to house. Each family was required to keep a bucket and ladder on hand in case a blaze broke out. If a house did catch fire, everyone helped put out the flames.

GOING AND COMING

Roads in the thirteen colonies were notoriously bad, when they existed at all. In the early days most people traveled by water if they had a choice. In the 1700s stagecoach lines began to carry passengers between major cities. A trip by coach was a big improvement over travel on foot or horseback. But it was still slow and thoroughly uncomfortable.

THE GENIUS OF PHILADELPHIA

Without question the most famous citizen of the Middle Colonies was Benjamin Franklin (1706–1780). Franklin moved to Philadelphia from Boston when he was seventeen. He was a man with many interests and talents. He experimented with electricity. He invented the rocking chair, the Franklin stove, and many other useful things. During the War of Independence he helped persuade France to aid the American cause. Franklin never forgot his adopted city. He gave Philadelphia its first lending library and its first volunteer fire department.

Benjamin Franklin flew a kite during a thunderstorm and proved that lightning is electricity. Franklin wore many hats: he was a printer, writer, postmaster, inventor, scientist, and diplomat.

Stagecoaches were usually crowded and stuffy.
An inn was a welcome sight for many a weary traveler.

At night the coach travelers stopped at inns along the road. "We generally reached our resting-place for the night if no accident intervened, at ten o'clock," one traveler wrote, describing a trip from Boston to New York: "After a frugal supper [we] went to bed, with a notice that we should be called at three next morning, which generally proved to be half-past two, and then, whether it snowed or rained, the traveler must rise and make ready, by the help of a horn-lantern and a farthing candle, and proceed on his way over bad roads, sometimes getting out to help the coachman lift the coach out of a quagmire or rut, and arrive in New York after a week's hard traveling."

The bad roads did nothing to help the colonists send and receive letters. If you wanted to send a letter during the 1600s you probably waited until you met someone who happened to be traveling in the right direction. In 1710 the British government established a colonial postal system with New York as its center. Very gradually a reliable service developed. By 1715 a rider carried letters between Philadelphia and New York once a week. On the way he stopped at Burlington, Perth Amboy, and other towns in New Jersey. He left Philadelphia every Friday morning and arrived in New York on Saturday night.

The colonial post rider took pride in his job, and people were glad to have the weekly mail service.

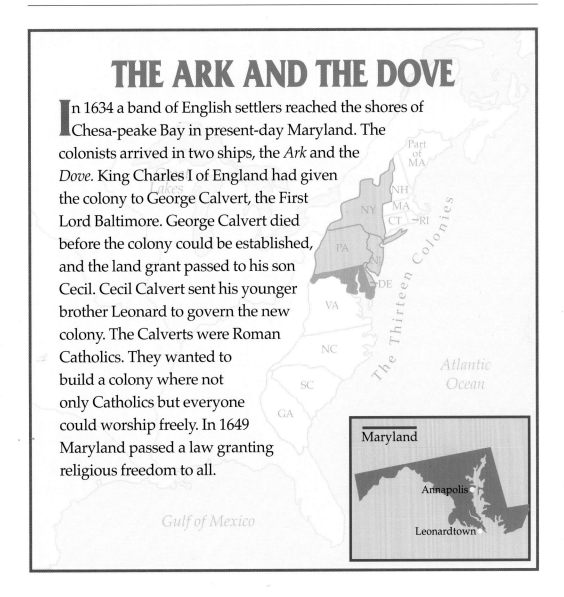

THE ARK AND THE DOVE

In 1634 a band of English settlers reached the shores of Chesa-peake Bay in present-day Maryland. The colonists arrived in two ships, the *Ark* and the *Dove*. King Charles I of England had given the colony to George Calvert, the First Lord Baltimore. George Calvert died before the colony could be established, and the land grant passed to his son Cecil. Cecil Calvert sent his younger brother Leonard to govern the new colony. The Calverts were Roman Catholics. They wanted to build a colony where not only Catholics but everyone could worship freely. In 1649 Maryland passed a law granting religious freedom to all.

Part of MA

NH

Lakes

NY   MA

CT—RI

PA

NJ

DE

VA

NC

SC

GA

The Thirteen Colonies

Atlantic Ocean

Gulf of Mexico

Maryland

Annapolis

Leonardtown

The colonial mail carrier was known as the post rider because he usually traveled on horseback. But horses could not travel when deep snow buried the roads and trails. In New York mail carriers found a clever solution. When the Hudson River froze solid, the post rider skated back and forth all the way from New York City to Albany.

Skating served practical purposes, but it was also a pure pleasure. Gliding on the ice was one of the many entertainments that enriched the lives of the people in the Middle Colonies.

6
When the Day's Work Was Done

"Their diversion in winter is riding sleighs about three or four miles out of town where they have houses of entertainment at a place called the Bowery, and some go to friends' houses, who handsomely treat them.... I believe we met fifty or sixty sleighs that day. They fly with great swiftness and some are so furious that they will turn out of the path for none except a loaded cart."

—SARAH KEMBLE KNIGHT, A VISITOR TO NEW YORK, 1704

MAKING MERRY

Most people in the Middle Colonies worked hard six days a week. Sunday, their day of rest, was devoted to church services and Bible reading. Nevertheless the colonists found time to dance and make music. They painted, embroidered, and developed an array of crafts. Whether they lived in town or in the country, they got together for special occasions. The colonists found a host of ways to have fun.

Arts and entertainment varied widely in the Middle Colonies. The Dutch of New Netherland loved to sit in taverns, drinking beer, trading stories, and singing jolly songs. The Pennsylvania Quakers were more subdued. Their parties were quieter, but they had plenty of good food and good fellowship.

A formal ball was an exciting event, usually reserved for wealthier colonists.

JOLLY OLD SAINT NICHOLAS

Dutch children in the colonies delighted in a custom they brought from the Netherlands. On December 5 they left their shoes out at night to be filled with treats from Saint Nicholas. Saint Nicholas stuffed the shoes with candy, fruit, and small toys. Today Saint Nicholas still visits children in the United States. Now he arrives on Christmas in the form of Santa Claus.

In Maryland, where farms or "plantations" were widely scattered, people gathered for formal dances or balls. A visitor described a ball that took place in Annapolis in 1744:

"The ladies of note made a splendid appearance. In a room back from where they danced were several sorts of wines, punch and sweetmeats. In this room those that were not engaged in any dancing match might better employ themselves at cards, dice, backgammon, or with a cheerful glass.… With a mutual consent about 2 of the clock in the morning it was agreed to break up, every gentleman waiting on his partner home."

In New York and Philadelphia fishing parties were popular get-togethers for young people. A visitor from England gives this account of a typical party held in 1759:

"Thirty or forty gentlemen and ladies meet and dine together, drink tea in the afternoon, fish and amuse themselves till evening and then return home.… In the way there is a bridge, about three miles distant from New York which you always pass over as you return, called the Kissing Bridge where it is a part of the etiquette to salute the lady who has put herself under your protection."

Balls and fishing parties were reserved for people of wealth and position in the colonies. Slaves, indentured servants, and apprentices had no such pleasures. They snatched whatever moments they could for relaxation and fun. Sometimes work itself provided the chance for a party. At harvesttime whole families, servants and all, went to help their neighbors. In the same way people gathered to help build a barn, stitch together a quilt, or husk mounded ears of corn.

New York and Philadelphia remained centers for entertainment. But by the 1700s the world was growing wider. Country people did not often get to the cities. But sometimes entertainment reached their villages and farms.

Quilting bees were popular with colonial women. There they could visit with friends and make a beautiful quilt at the same time.

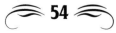

THE SHOW MUST GO ON!

People in colonial villages didn't see many strangers. When a traveling show came to town, no one wanted to miss the excitement. Colonists in New York saw their first traveling stage play in about 1700. In 1724 a ropedancer and a clown called Pickle Herring delighted audiences in southeastern Pennsylvania. Some traveling shows included acrobats, puppeteers, and exotic animals such as lions or giraffes.

Scientific shows were very popular in the 1700s. The "scientist" would call a child from the audience for a demonstration. With the use of "electrical fluid," the scientist made the child's hair stand on end. Such traveling exhibitions inspired Benjamin Franklin to conduct ground-breaking experiments with electricity.

Many church and town officials opposed shows of any kind. In 1700 Pennsylvania's legislature passed a law against "stage plays, masques, [and] revels, as well as rude and riotous sport." But the British government overturned this and similar laws. Finally, in 1754, Philadelphia got its first theater. The theater's organizers promised to present only plays of the highest moral quality.

In one way or another, music was available throughout the colonies. People sang in taverns and barbershops. They gathered in drawing rooms to hear young ladies and gentlemen play the violin or the flute. Long church services were enlivened with the singing of hymns.

Some of the Pennsylvania Germans raised hymn singing to an art form. The members of the Ephrata Cloister composed more than a thousand sacred songs. Choirs at Ephrata developed a unique style. Members sang falsetto with the lips almost closed. According to one member of the group, this unusual method "throws the sound up to the ceiling and the melody, which seems to be more than human, appears to be descending from above and hovering over the heads of the assembly."

Before dawn on Easter Sunday the Moravians formed a procession and walked to the cemetery. As they walked they sang hymns, accompanied by flutes, violins, trumpets, and other instruments. In 1748 the Moravians

THE POWER OF MUSIC

On December 24, 1755, Indians massacred the Moravian mission at Gnadenhutten, Pennsylvania. Refugees fled to the nearby village of Bethlehem. The Native Americans surrounded the village, preparing for another attack. Early on the morning of December 25 a lone musician climbed to a Bethlehem rooftop. He played carols on his trombone to celebrate Christmas Day. The Indians thought the colonists were calling on powerful magic. They turned away in fear and left Bethlehem unharmed.

started the first symphony orchestra in the British colonies. It had fourteen members. Today the Moravians are recognized for their lasting contribution to American music.

PICTURING THE WORLD

Among the travelers who visited colonial towns and farmhouses were itinerant portrait painters. These artists, or "limners," carried bundles of canvases with partially completed pictures. When someone agreed to have a portrait done, the limner simply filled in the face. Some artists advertised their services. In 1752 a Maryland newspaper ran a notice for a painter who would do anything "in the limning way, history, altarpieces for churches, landscapes, views of…houses and estates, signs, or any other way of painting and also gilding."

A few painters from the Middle Colonies stand out for their achievements. Gustavus Hesselius came to Wilmington, Delaware, from Sweden in 1712. He traveled through Delaware, Maryland, and Pennsylvania, painting portraits, landscapes, and religious works. He is also remembered for his paintings of Native Americans. Benjamin West was born in Phila-

Ammi Phillips was a well-known limner of the time.
Among his works, there are several portraits of little girls
wearing the same bright-red dress.

In 1735, Gustavus Hesselius painted this portrait of a Native American chief.

delphia in 1738. By the time he was fifteen he was an excellent portrait painter. West left for Europe in 1760 and never returned to the New World.

Painting was not the only form of art practiced by the colonists. Some made beautiful ceramic tiles to decorate hearths and fireplaces. These tiles,

This chest made by Pennsylvania Germans was decorated with mermaids and flowers. Made for a newly married woman, Anne Beer, it also includes the date of her wedding.

painted with biblical scenes, were very popular in New York and New Jersey. Crafts such as quilting and weaving were also a means of artistic expression. Colonial women did beautiful embroidery on dresses and cushions. Girls learned to embroider by making wall hangings known as samplers. Into the sampler the girl stitched a Bible verse such as "God is love," illustrated with hearts, doves, or flowers.

One nearly forgotten colonial craft is paper cutting. Colonial women and girls cut intricate patterns into gold or silver paper. Sometimes they added delicate stitching with thread or strands of hair. Paper cuts were sometimes given as gifts by a girl to her lover.

In the early days of the Middle Colonies, people thought of themselves as Dutch, Swedish, German, French, or English. They clung to their Old World languages and customs. Over the years the colonists intermarried, setting their cultural differences aside. They began to think of themselves not as transplanted Europeans, but as Americans.

There were special schools that taught girls how to stitch beautiful samplers like this. The young lady who made this was thirteen years old.

In 1776 leaders from the thirteen British colonies gathered in Philadelphia. There they signed the document known as the Declaration of Independence. The Middle Colonies joined their sisters to the north and south to form a new nation. The colonial era was at an end, and a new age had begun.

Glossary

alcove: A small, closetlike space.

apprentice: A person contracted to work for a master or mistress for several years in order to learn a trade.

asset: Something valuable or useful; advantage.

attire: Clothing and accessories.

backlog: A large, heavy log placed at the back of a fireplace.

celibate: Without a spouse or mate.

cockade: An ornamental knot of ribbon worn on a hat.

court-martial: To put on a trial before a military court.

dandy: A gentleman who liked to wear fancy clothes.

defame: To unjustly damage a person's reputation.

falsetto: Sung by artificially forcing the voice beyond its normal upper range.

farthing: English coin (no longer used) worth one-fourth of a penny.

flax: A plant whose fibers are used for making linen thread.

garret: Attic.

indenture: The contract by which a person was bound as a servant for a given number of years.

itinerant: Traveling from place to place.

jaunt: A short trip, usually at a brisk pace.

masque: A dramatic entertainment popular in the sixteenth and seventeenth centuries; it was usually based on mythic themes and performed by masked actors.

notorious: Famous for bad behavior.

pewter: A gray metal made by blending a small amount of copper and antimony with tin.

plane: To smooth a rough surface by scraping or polishing.

pomade: Perfumed oil for the hair.

quagmire: Soft marshy land.

revel: Wild party.

Sabbath: The seventh day of the week—Sunday for most Christians—observed as a day of rest and worship.

sapling: Slender young tree.

Scandinavia: Peninsula in northern Europe made up of Norway, Sweden, Denmark, and parts of Finland.

sect: A religious group that has separated from the religion of which it was a part. Members of a sect share the same beliefs and practices.

stronghold: Seat of power.

thatch: To cover a roof with plant material, such as straw or reeds, for insulation.

trencher: A wooden platter used as a plate for food.

A NOTE ABOUT SPELLING

If you were to read a letter or diary written in colonial days, you would be amazed by the way some of the words are spelled. The word wind might be spelled wynd or wynde. Words would be capitalized almost at random. Until the middle of the 1700s, English-language spelling had few standard rules. People spelled words more or less as they wished. The results are certainly interesting, but they can be confusing, too. To clarify the meaning for the readers of this book, I have modernized the spelling in all quotes from colonial documents.

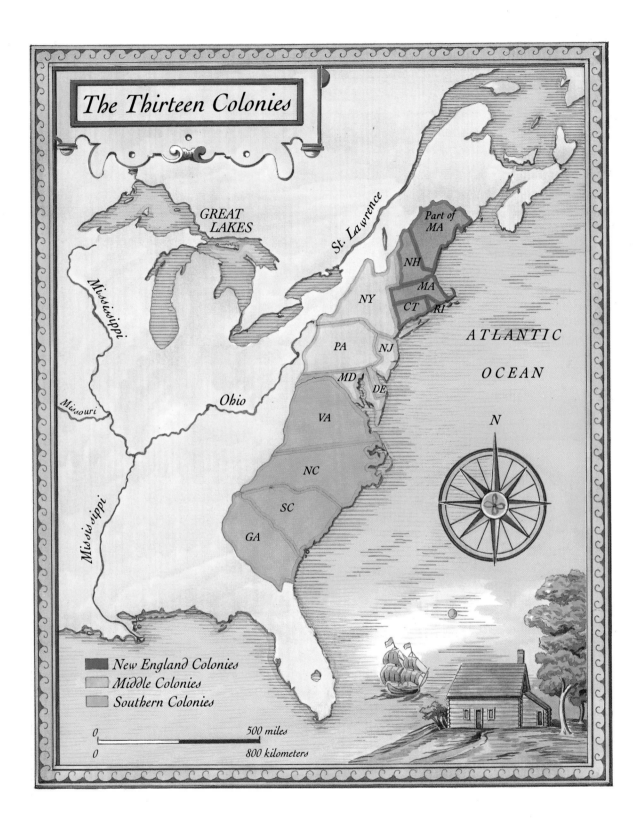

The Thirteen Colonies

GREAT LAKES

St. Lawrence

Mississippi

Missouri

Ohio

Mississippi

Part of MA

NH

MA

NY

CT

RI

PA

NJ

MD

DE

VA

NC

SC

GA

ATLANTIC

OCEAN

N

New England Colonies
Middle Colonies
Southern Colonies

0   500 miles

0   800 kilometers

The Middle Colonies in Time

1609—Henry Hudson, a British captain sailing under the Dutch flag, discovers the river that today bears his name; he claims the Hudson River region for the Netherlands.

1624—Dutch fur traders found Fort Orange at present-day Albany.

1626—Peter Minuit buys Manhattan Island from the Indians.

about 1630—The Dutch establish a settlement at Pavonia near present-day Jersey City; it is destroyed by Indian attack, but other Dutch settlements spring up in the region.

1634—Maryland is founded when English colonists establish St. Mary's City on the western shore of Chesapeake Bay.

1638—Swedish settlers establish New Sweden on Delaware Bay in present-day New Jersey and Delaware.

1655—The Dutch seize control of New Sweden.

1664—The British capture New Netherland from the Dutch.

1682—William Penn and his Quaker followers found Pennsylvania with their settlement at Philadelphia.

1689—England goes to war with France and its Indian allies; this is the first of a series of conflicts called the French and Indian Wars.

1710—The British government authorizes a colonial postal system to be based in New York City.

1748—The Moravians of Pennsylvania establish the first symphony orchestra in the thirteen colonies.

1754–1763—The last of the French and Indian Wars deprives France of much of its North American territory.

1776—Colonial leaders gather in Philadelphia to sign the Declaration of Independence, severing the ties between Great Britain and the thirteen colonies.

1783—The Treaty of Paris ends the American Revolution; the United States of America becomes an independent nation.

Places to Visit

DELAWARE

Fort Christina Monument, Wilmington:
This monument marks the site of
Delaware's original Swedish settlement.
On the grounds stands a replica of a
colonial log cabin.

Old Swedes Church, Wilmington:
Built by Swedish immigrants in 1698, this is
one of the oldest churches in the United States.

MARYLAND

St. Mary's City, Leonardtown:
This is the reconstruction of a village that
dates back to 1634. The site includes a recon-
structed tobacco plantation and a replica of
the Dove, one of the ships that brought the
first English settlers to Maryland.

William Paca House, Annapolis:
William Paca was one of the proprietors of
colonial Maryland. His home has been fully
restored with furnishings of the time.

NEW JERSEY

Old Barracks, Trenton:
During a series of wars with France and its
Indian allies the British used this fort between
1689 and 1763. A museum displays cannons,
rifles, and other relics of the fighting.

Waterloo Village, Stanhope:
Waterloo Village has been carefully recon-
structed to show how people lived during
the 1700s. Among the attractions are a colonial gristmill, a working blacksmith shop,
and several homes with colonial furnishings.

NEW YORK

Fort Niagara, Youngstown:
This British fort played a key role in colonial defenses during the French and Indian
War (1754–1763). It has been restored to
look much as it did during colonial times.

Fraunces Tavern, New York City:
This tavern was a popular meeting place
during the 1770s. After the American
Revolution, General George Washington
came here to bid his officers farewell.
Fraunces Tavern is still open for business
after more than two hundred years.

PENNSYLVANIA

Ephrata Cloister, Lancaster:
Ten original buildings from this religious
community have been restored. Ephrata
was founded in 1732 and survived until
the early 1800s.

Pennsbury Manor, Bucks County:
Pennsbury was the home and farm of
William Penn. It was built on land that
he bought from the Indians in 1682.
Pennsbury has been fully restored.

To Learn More...

BOOKS

Hakim, Joy. *Making Thirteen Colonies.*
New York: Oxford University Press, 1993.

Kent, Deborah. *Benjamin Franklin: Extraordinary Patriot.* New York: Scholastic, 1993.

Madison, Arnold. *How the Colonists Lived.*
New York: McKay, 1981.

Reische, Diana. *Founding the American Colonies.* New York: Franklin Watts, 1989.

Scott, John A. *Settlers on the Eastern Shore.*
New York: Facts on File, 1991.

Smith, Carter, ed. *Daily Life: A Sourcebook on Colonial America.* Brookfield, CT:
Millbrook, 1992.

Tunis, Edwin. *Colonial Living.* New York:
Crowell, 1975.

Warner, John F. *Colonial American Home Life.*
New York: Franklin Watts, 1993.

Washburne, Carolyn Kott. *A Multicultural Portrait of Colonial Life.* Tarrytown, NY:
Marshall Cavendish, 1994.

WEBSITES*

Pennsylvania Memories Last a Lifetime,
Click on Pennsylvania History and get
information from the Pennsylvania
Historical Museum Commission.
http://www.state.pa.us/welcome.html

*Websites change from time to time. For additional on-line information, check with your media specialist at your local library.

Bibliography

Bailyn, Bernard. *The Peopling of British North America: An Introduction.* New York: Knopf, 1986.

Bridenbaugh, Carl. *Cities in the Wilderness: The First Century of Urban Life in America, 1625–1742.* 2d ed. New York: Oxford University Press, 1971.

Earle, Alice Morse. *Child Life in Colonial Days.* Stockbridge, MA: Berkshire House, 1993. (Originally published by Macmillan, New York, 1899.)

———. *Colonial Dames and Good Wives.* New York: Frederick Ungar, 1962.

———. *Colonial Days in Old New York.* New York: Empire State Publishing, 1926. (Originally published by Scribner, New York, 1896.)

———. *Home Life in Colonial Days.* Stockbridge, MA: Berkshire House, 1993. (Originally published by Macmillan, New York, 1898.)

Encyclopedia Britannica, ed. *The Annals of America.* Vol. 1, *Discovering a New World 1493–1754.* Chicago: Encyclopedia Britannica, 1976.

Hawke, David Freeman. *Everyday Life in Early America.* New York: Harper & Row, 1988.

Langdon, William Chauncy. *Everyday Things in Early America, 1607–1776.* New York: Scribners, 1938.

Nash, Gary B. *Red, White, and Black: The Peoples of Early America.* 3d ed. Englewood Cliffs, NJ: Prentice-Hall, 1992.

Rae, Noel, ed. *Witnessing America: The Library of Congress Book of Firsthand Accounts of Life in America, 1600–1900.* New York: Penguin, 1996.

Reisch, Jerome R. *Colonial America.* Englewood Cliffs, NJ: Prentice-Hall, 1994.

Starkey, Marion L. *Land Where Our Fathers Died: The Settling of the Eastern Shores, 1607–1735.* New York: Doubleday, 1962.

Train, Arthur, Jr. *The Story of Everyday Things.* New York: Harper & Brothers, 1941.

Wright, Lewis B. *The Cultural Life of the American Colonies, 1607–1763.* New York: Harper & Row, 1957.

Notes on Quotes

The quotations from this book are from
the following sources:

New Voices in a Strange Land
Page 7,"The air was sweet": Starkey,
Land Where Our Fathers Died: p. 140.

At Home in Town and Country
Page 11,"The Dutch here keep their houses
very neat and clean": Rae, *Witnessing America,*
p. 229.

Page 15,"I wish thee could see our big kitchen":
Land Where Our Fathers Died, p. 192.

Page 17,"The hair is loaded with powder and
pomade": Train, *The Story of Everyday Things,*
p. 192.

Boys and Girls Together
Page 21,"I have not read of any virtue":
Earle, *Child Life in Colonial Days,* p. 196.

Page 23,"Ran away: A servant": *Child Life
in Colonial Days,* p. 72.

Page 23,"demean himself patient" and"beat
each other and tore the clothes": *Child Life in
Colonial Days,* p. 202.

Page 24,"I went to Madame B.'s exhibition":
Child Life in Colonial Days, p. 115.

Page 24,"This indenture witnesses":
Encyclopedia Britannica. *The Annals of
America,* Vol. 1, p. 335.

Page 27,"Some people in Philadelphia have
tamed beavers": *Witnessing America,* p. 256.

Ways of Worship
Page 31,"God, through Christ, has placed
a principle in every man": *The Annals of America,*
Vol.1, p. 299.

Page 33,"This plain Friend and his plain
though pretty wife": *The Story of Everyday
Things,* p. 195.

Page 37,"Many Jews have settled in New York":
Wright, *The Cultural Life of the American
Colonies,* pp. 64-65.

Page 38,"the ordinary and customary labors"
and"dancing, card-playing, tick-tacking":
Earle, *Colonial Days in Old New York,* p. 262.

Problems and Solutions
Page 41,"No person shall strip the fences":
Colonial Days in Old New York, p. 253.

Page 42,"a common scold may be indicted":
Earle, *Colonial Dames and Good Wives,* p. 92.

Page 43,"the said Melchoir Classen shall run
the gantlope": *Colonial Days in Old New York,*
pp. 244-245.

Page 47,"We generally reached our resting-
place": Earle, *Home Life in Colonial Days,* p. 347.

When the Day's Work Was Done
Page 51,"Their diversion in winter is riding
sleighs": *Colonial Dames and Good Wives,*
p. 217.

Page 53,"The ladies of note": *Colonial Dames and Good Wives,* p. 210.

Page 53,"Thirty or forty gentlemen and ladies": *Colonial Dames and Good Wives,* p. 218.

Page 55,"stage plays, masques, revels": *The Cultural Life of the American Colonies,* p. 179.

Page 55,"throws the sound up to the ceiling": Langdon, *Everyday Things in Early America, 1607–1776,* p. 84.

Page 56, do anything "in the limning way": *The Cultural Life of the American Colonies,* p. 213.

Index

About the Author

Deborah Kent grew up in Little Falls, New Jersey, and received her Bachelor of Arts degree from Oberlin College in Ohio. She went on to earn a Master's Degree from Smith College School for Social Work and took a job at the University Settlement House in New York City. After four years in social work, she decided to pursue her lifelong interest in writing. She moved to San Miguel de Allende, Mexico, a charming town with a colony of foreign writers and artists. In San Miguel she wrote her first novel for young adults, *Belonging*.

Today Deborah has more than a dozen novels to her credit, and has written many nonfiction children's books as well. She lives in Chicago with her husband, children's book author R. Conrad Stein, and their daughter, Janna.

"When I was in school," Deborah recalls, "I thought history was boring. We learned about wars and political leaders, but seldom heard about ordinary people. Back then I could never have guessed that some day I would study history for fun, and that I would even write books about it! I am fascinated not by generals and presidents, but by the women, men, and children of the past whose names have been nearly forgotten. It is exciting to explore the world they knew and to try to imagine how they lived their lives."